Looking At Te[ddy Bears]

by Sallie Purkis

Contents

New teddy bears	2
Sarah's teddies	4
Jean's bear	6
Older bears	8
Oldest bears	10
Two famous teddy bears	12
Teddy bears in museums	14
Index	16

New teddy bears

Joseph is a new baby.
Joseph has a new teddy bear.
Gran bought teddy the day
Joseph was born.

New teddies feel soft.

When they get dirty they go in the washing machine.

Sarah's teddies

Sarah has lots of teddies.
Some are new.
Some are old.

Here's Sarah with her mum, Sally. Sally is holding the teddy bear she had when she was a baby.
The teddy is as old as Sally.

Jean's bear

Jean's bear is even older
than Sally's bear.
His fur has come out.
He feels hard,
not soft.

You can't wash Jean's bear
in the washing machine.

When Jean was young, teddy was a new bear.
Look at him in this picture.
Teddy is the same age as Jean.

Older bears

This bear is older than Jean's bear. He's over eighty years old. Look at his long arms and pointed snout. Inside he's full of sawdust and feels very hard.

German bear dressed as World War I sailor

These old bears are clockwork bears. You wind them up with a key to make them move.
This bear rides on roller skates.

German, Bing, 1920

German, Schuco, c. 1909

These two bears walk.

Oldest bears

Here is one of the oldest bears ever made.
Very old bears are more like real bears.
They have humps on their backs, long arms and tiny black eyes.
Some even make a growling noise when you press them.

Rare Steiff Bear, c.1905

This is what a real bear looks like.

Two famous teddy bears

This man wrote a story about the teddy in the picture.
His son Christopher Robin called the bear "Pooh Bear".
A A Milne's stories of Pooh Bear are famous.

Alan Alexander Milne with his son Christopher Robin, 1926

A writer called Michael Bond wrote stories about a teddy bear called "Paddington". He bought the bear from a shop in London. Children enjoyed the stories so much that many more teddy bears like Paddington were sold.

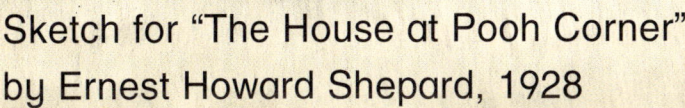

Sketch for "The House at Pooh Corner" by Ernest Howard Shepard, 1928

Teddy bears in museums

Pauline works in a museum. She looks at lots of old bears.
Some are soft.
Some are hard.
Some have long arms.
Some have short arms.
Some can growl.
Pauline uses these clues to tell her how old each bear is.

This is a very special teddy bear museum at Stratford-upon-Avon.

Index

arms 8, 10, 14
baby 2
clockwork bears 9
eyes 10
fur 6
growl 10, 14
humps 10
key 9
museum 14, 15
Paddington Bear 13
Pooh Bear 12

real bears 10, 11
roller skates 9
sawdust 8
shop 13
snout 8
stories 12, 13
washing machine 3, 6